David Downie

LLB(hons) BSc(hons)
Former partner, McCullough Robertson

INDEMNITY AND EXCLUSION CLAUSES

DAVID DOWNIE

A practical approach under Australian law

INDEMNITY AND EXCLUSION CLAUSES: A PRACTICAL
APPROACH UNDER AUSTRALIAN LAW

The author acknowledges being influenced by the thinking of leading
Australian academic Professor John Carter in his various publications over the
past seventeen years.

Published by Inter Alia Publishing

CONTENTS

What is an indemnity.. 1

Interaction with contractual principles 5

How are indemnities construed? 10

Reflexive indemnities 15

Civil Liability legislation 27

Drafting and negotiating indemnities 29

Why exclusion clauses are important............................... 34

How exclusion clauses are interpreted............................. 36

Consequential loss 47

Australian Consumer Law 53

Practical tips 56

WHAT IS AN INDEMNITY

To indemnify or to give an indemnity is a very serious commitment. It is, in effect, offering to hold someone harmless should a particular event occur (much in the same way an insurer does.) The event need not have been caused by any wrong by the indemnifying party (in fact it may have been caused by the indemnified party). The amount claimable under an indemnity may not be limited by the usual common law requirement of remoteness, or any requirement of the indemnified to mitigate loss. The indemnity may not be subject to any limitation or exclusion under the agreement.

Hence an indemnity is, at least in theory, an excellent mechanism for passing risk with respect to an event to another party to an agreement. Given this, the terms of an indemnity should never be considered 'standard', and should be carefully considered by both the indemnifier and the indemnified before it is agreed to.

TYPES OF INDEMNITIES

There is no set form for an indemnity. However, the three types of indemnities that are seen frequently in practice are:

- where Party A indemnifies Party B for claims by Party C;
- where Party A indemnifies Party B for breach of contract by Party A; and

- where Party A indemnifies Party B for claims made by Party A due to the negligence of or breach of contract by Party B.

It is important to note that an indemnity can arise on any event specified in the contract – it is not limited to these examples.

Case example

The Codemasters Software Co Ltd v Automobile Club de L'Ouest (ACO) **[2009] EWHC 2361 (Ch) and [2009] EWHC 3194 (Ch)**

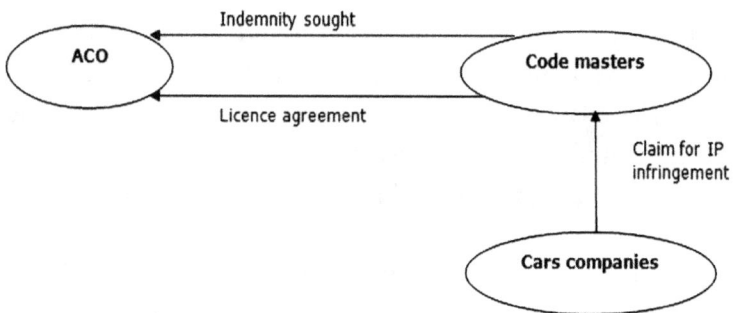

ACO was the organiser of a series of car races, known as the Le Mans series. Codemasters designed computer games and wanted to include in one of their games representations of the Le Mans series as well as some of the car brands which took part.

ACO and Codemasters entered into a non–exclusive licensing agreement, in which ACO appeared to grant Codemasters the right to use the car designs, manufacturers' names etc of participants in the 2006 series. The cars to be featured in Codemasters' game included Porsche, Ferrari and Lamborghini.

Upon release of a promotional video for the game, Porsche, Ferrari and Lamborghini each claimed Codemasters had infringed their intellectual property, as ACO had no right to grant licences of their trade marks and designs. Codemasters agreed to remove Ferrari's cars from the game, reached settlement with Lamborghini and was still negotiating a settlement with Porsche.

Codemasters commenced proceedings against ACO, seeking an indemnity against the claims of the three car brands, relying on the following clause:

'10.1 *ACO represents, warrants and covenants to Codemasters that:*

(i) *[it] has the right… to grant all rights and licenses which it is granting under this Agreement, free, clear and unencumbered, and without violating or breaching the legal equitable or contractual rights of any person anywhere in the world;*

(ii) *the use and reproduction of the Endorsements as authorised hereunder will not infringe, violate or breach any intellectual or industrial property or moral right (or any rights of a similar nature) anywhere in the world.*

10.3 *Each party (the 'Indemnifying Party') will **indemnify, defend and hold harmless** the other party and its affiliates, parent companies, subsidiaries, and their respective directors, officers and employees, from any and all claims, causes of action, suits, damages or demands whatsoever, arising out of any breach or alleged breach of any agreement or warranty made by the indemnifying Party pursuant to this Agreement.'*

The cases consisted of two temporary decisions. The latter interim decision contained some observations about the principles governing the Codemasters' claim for an indemnity from ACO.

ACO claimed that the indemnity only applied to breaches of the agreement by the parties, not to third party claims (that is, a 'party–party' indemnity). The Court rejected this argument and held that the use of the word 'defend' in the indemnity clause necessitated the conclusion that the indemnity covered claims by some other party against the party indemnified, which included the claims by the Porsche, Ferrari and Lamborghini.

As Codemasters won on the point of law, they were awarded their costs of the interlocutory application (£70,000).

INTERACTION WITH CONTRACTUAL PRINCIPLES

The extent to which general contract law principles (such as mitigation and remoteness) apply to the measure of an indemnified party's loss under an indemnity is unclear.

One view of an indemnity is that it operates by way of prevention of a loss. This means that, by promising to hold another 'harmless', a breach of contract occurs when the indemnified party suffers loss. The competing view is that indemnities operate by requiring the indemnified party to be made whole once the loss has been suffered. This means that, when the indemnified party suffers loss, no breach of contract has occurred, but the indemnifier now has obligation to compensate the indemnified party for its loss (and will breach the contract if it does not).

It may be that whether an indemnity is a 'prevent—loss' indemnity or a requirement to compensate once loss has occurred is a matter of the intention of the parties (i.e. construction of the indemnity). It would be absurd for example to think that an insurer would be in breach of contract on the occurrence of the event insured against. Similarly, a Court would presumably give effect to a promise to hold someone from harm if the intention of the parties was clear.

A further consideration is whether or not a claim under an indemnity is a claim for damages due to breach, a claim for a liquidated or unliquidated debt, or something else. Indemnity cases tend not to look at the ordinary contractual damages principles when considering a claim under an indemnity (such as causation, remoteness and mitigation).[1] This suggests that a claim under an indemnity is not a claim for damages following a breach of contract.

Even if this were correct, it does not mean that a Court will not impose limitations on amounts recoverable under an indemnity (as they would if general law damages principles applied). For example, if an indemnified party settles a claim with a third party, it is generally accepted that the settlement reached between the parties must be reasonable.[2]

One justification for this position is that an unreasonable settlement would not follow from the relevant event under the terms of the indemnity. In *General Feeds Inc Panama v Slobodna Plovidba Yugoslavia* [1999] 1 Lloyd Rep 688 at 691–2, Colman J stated:

> '...the overall exercise which the Court must do is to consider whether the specified eventuality (in the case of an indemnity)... has caused the loss incurred in satisfying the settlement. Unless the claim is of sufficient strength reasonably to justify a settlement and the amount paid in settlement is reasonable having regard to the strength of the claim, it cannot be shown that the loss has been caused by the relevant eventuality or breach of contract.'

---

[1]   Wayne Courtney and J W Carter, *Indemnities against breach and settlements of third party claims*, (2011) 27 Journal of Contract Law

[2]   *Unity Insurance Brokers Pty Ltd v Rocco Pezzano Pty Ltd* (1998) 192 CLR 603

As a more general perspective is that, as a matter of construction, there is an implied limitation on the indemnity.[3] What loss did the parties intend to be recoverable?

In *White Industries Qld Pty Ltd v Hennessy Glass & Aluminium Systems Pty Ltd* [1999] 1 Qd R 210 at 226–7, Derrington J stated:

> '...the contractual promise is, in effect, to save the contractor from any loss to it following from the prescribed factor, and the contractor's obligation under the settlement to pay the agreed amount is a loss of that description and as such it attracts the indemnity. As a controlling measure, by implication from the nature of the promise, and associated with the duty of an indemnified party to take all reasonable steps to protect the interests of the indemnifying party in respect of the transaction, there is a qualification that the settlement must be reasonable.'

A similar position was taken in the United Kingdom case of the *Codemasters'* case. In this case, the Court stated that:

> '[W]hether one regards it as an aspect of the law of the interpretation of contracts or whether one regards it as an aspect of the law of causation and quantification of damages...it follows...that in order to recover the sums which Codemasters seek to recover, which Codemasters say arise out of the claims made by Lamborghini, Ferrari and Porsche, then Codemasters must prove that any settlements entered into with those third parties are reasonable.
>
> It also follows...that clause 10.3, whatever its true construction, does not mean that Codemasters can claim an indemnity in

---

[3] Wayne Courtney and J W Carter, *indemnities against breach and settlements of third party claims*, (2011) 27 Journal of Contract Law

> *respect of unreasonable settlements, for example, a settlement by*
> *Codemasters entered into for an inflated sum.'*

While mitigation as a principle was not found to be relevant in determining the scope of the indemnity in *Codemasters*, the Court acknowledged that this did not necessarily rule out the same result being achieved by another route. In many cases, the requirement that the settlement be reasonable will have the same result as if the principle of mitigation was applied.

As to whether the contractual principle of remoteness is applicable, the authorities are less clear. The general view is that the test of remoteness as set down in *Hadley v Baxendale* (1854) 9 Ex 341 does not apply to indemnities – the indemnity cases tend not to apply it. However, as a matter of construction, it is arguable that the remoteness concept may have some application if the type of loss suffered by the indemnified party was not in the parties' contemplation as a relevant kind to arise from the event giving rise to the indemnity.[4]

The reverse argument is that when parties agree to an indemnity, they often do so on the presumption that an indemnity would give rise to a more *extensive* liability that under common law principles. Therefore, to imply a concept of remoteness into an indemnity would defeat the parties' intentions.[5]

One thing that is clear is that this area of law is currently unsettled. As a result, parties should clarify that specific losses are recoverable if there is a particular concern, and, if giving an indemnity, it should be clarified that the indemnified party has an obligation to mitigate its loss.

---

[4]   Ibid
[5]   Ibid

Due to the uncertainty about how an indemnity is characterised (that is, whether a claim under an indemnity is a claim for breach of contract), parties should also expressly provide in their contracts whether or not amounts payable under an indemnity are subject to exclusions or limitations elsewhere in the agreement.

3

HOW ARE INDEMNITIES CONSTRUED?

Up until the case of *Andar Transport v Brambles* (2004) 217 CLR 424 there was a view that indemnities, like exclusion clauses, were to be interpreted using the approach from *Darlington Futures Ltd v Delco Australia Pty Ltd* (1986) 161 CLR 500. That is, they were to be given their natural and ordinary meaning read in light of the contract as a whole, and, where ambiguous, read against the person relying on them. However, following *Andar* things are less clear.

Andar Transport v Brambles (2004) 217 CLR 424

Sought indemnity

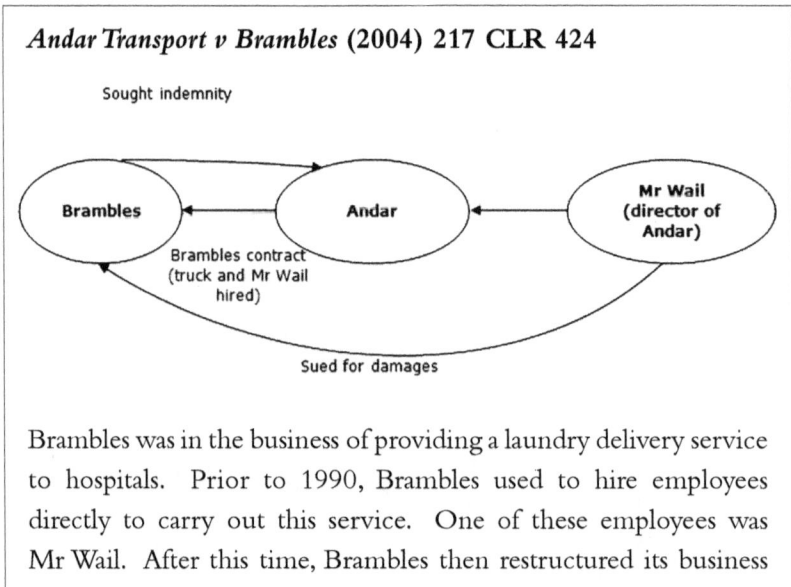

Brambles ← → Andar ← Mr Wail (director of Andar)

Brambles contract (truck and Mr Wail hired)

Sued for damages

Brambles was in the business of providing a laundry delivery service to hospitals. Prior to 1990, Brambles used to hire employees directly to carry out this service. One of these employees was Mr Wail. After this time, Brambles then restructured its business and required Mr Wail to carry out the delivery service as an independent contractor acting through a company. Mr Wail's company was named Andar.

Under the 'Independent Trucking Contractor Agreement' between Brambles and Andar, Andar was required to supply a specified truck and a suitably qualified driver, being Mr Wail (**Brambles Contract**).

Mr Wail injured his back while attempting to unload a trolley of linen from the truck. Mr Wail brought an action against Brambles. Brambles sought an indemnity from Andar (Mr Wail's company) under the Brambles Contract.

THE BRAMBLES CONTRACT

Andar provided two indemnities under the Brambles contract:

- xunder clause 4.6, Andar agreed:

'[t]o assume sole and entire responsibility for and indemnify [Brambles] against all claims liability losses expenses and damages arising from operation of the Vehicle by reason of any happening not attributable to the wilful negligent or malicious act or omission of [Brambles].

- Under clause 8, Andar agreed to indemnify Brambles from and against (among other things) all actions, claims, damages, proceedings and costs in respect of or arising from:

'...loss, damage, injury or accidental death from any cause to property or person caused or contributed to by the conduct of the Delivery Round by [Andar].' (clause 8.2.2); and

'...loss, damage, injury or accidental death from any cause to property or person occasioned or contributed to by any act, omission, neglect or breach or default of [Andar].' (clause 8.2.3)

The Victorian Court of Appeal held that Andar had also contributed to Mr Wail's injuries. Therefore, on a plain English reading of the indemnities in clause 8, the Court of Appeal held that Andar was liable to indemnify Brambles for Mr Wail's claim against Brambles.

On appeal, the High Court overturned this decision and held that the indemnity clauses in clause 8 did not extend to the negligence claim brought against Brambles.

THE HIGH COURT'S DECISION

In construing clause 8.2.2 and 8.2.3, the High Court found that (at [25]):

'...[N]either [of the clauses] expressly provides that liability arising on the part of Brambles as a result of injuries suffered to employees of Andar falls within the terms of the indemnity. That omission is not surprising.... [O]ne of the primary concerns of the Agreement is to ensure that, to outside observers, Brambles appears to be the sole entity involved in the provision of the relevant laundry services... The possibility of a suit against Brambles premised upon vicarious liability was, in the circumstances, a distinct possibility.'

The High Court also noted that:

- clause 8.2.2 was limited to liability arising in connection with the 'conduct of the Deliver Round by Andar', which could only occur through the driver, Mr Wail. As a result, the High Court found it unlikely that, in the absence of an express provision to the contrary, the parties intended that the indemnity would include injury to Mr Wail; and

- clause 8.2.3 referred to injury to a 'person' occasioned or contributed conduct of Andar, being the driver. The High Court found that the structure of the clause suggested that the 'person' in the first part of the clause was different to the person in the second part of the clause, being the driver (Mr Wail).

The High Court found that this construction was consistent with the indemnity given in clause 4.6 (extracted above).

To the extent that the indemnity was ambiguous, the High Court adopted the principle regarding indemnities as set out in *Ankar Pty Ltd v National Westminster Finance (Australia) Ltd* (1987) 162 CLR 549. *Ankar* was a case about contracts of guarantee which said that in a contract of guarantee, ambiguous contractual provisions should be construed in favour of the party giving the guarantee.

The High Court said (at [23]):

'...[N]otwithstanding the differences in the operation of guarantees and indemnities, both are designed to satisfy a liability owed to someone other than the guarantor or indemnifier to a third person. The principles adopted in Ankar...are therefore relevant to the construction of indemnity clauses.'

In the absence of a specific reference to claims by employees of Andar against Brambles, the Court read down the operation of the indemnity in favour of Andar.

13

The practical consequences of *Andar* include:

- understanding that indemnities are likely to be strictly construed, and that it is difficult to determine whether or not an indemnity will be applicable in any given factual situation;
- being as specific as possible when drafting to reduce the risk of the indemnity being read down, although you should assume the worst when reviewing and negotiating broad indemnities; and
- expressly referring to negligence if you wish the indemnity to apply in circumstances in which the indemnified party is negligent.

A party is still better off having indemnities in their favour than not.

4

REFLEXIVE INDEMNITIES

As contemplated by chapter 1, a class of indemnity exists called the 'reflexive indemnity' (sometimes called the 'reverse indemnity'). A reflexive indemnity exists where Party A agrees to indemnify Party B for claims made against Party B due the wrongdoing of Party B.

In the case of claims against Party B by Party A, such an indemnity can operate as an exclusion clause if the loss recoverable from Party A includes any loss in relation to the claim against Party B by Party A.

Understandably, the courts have generally been reluctant construe an indemnity clause as applying reflexively unless it is clear from both the wording of the indemnity clause and the contract as a whole that this was the parties' intention.

In *Qantas Airways Ltd v Aravco Ltd* (1996) 185 CLR 43, the language used was found to be unambiguous, and the indemnity clause required Aravco to indemnify Qantas for Qantas' own negligence.

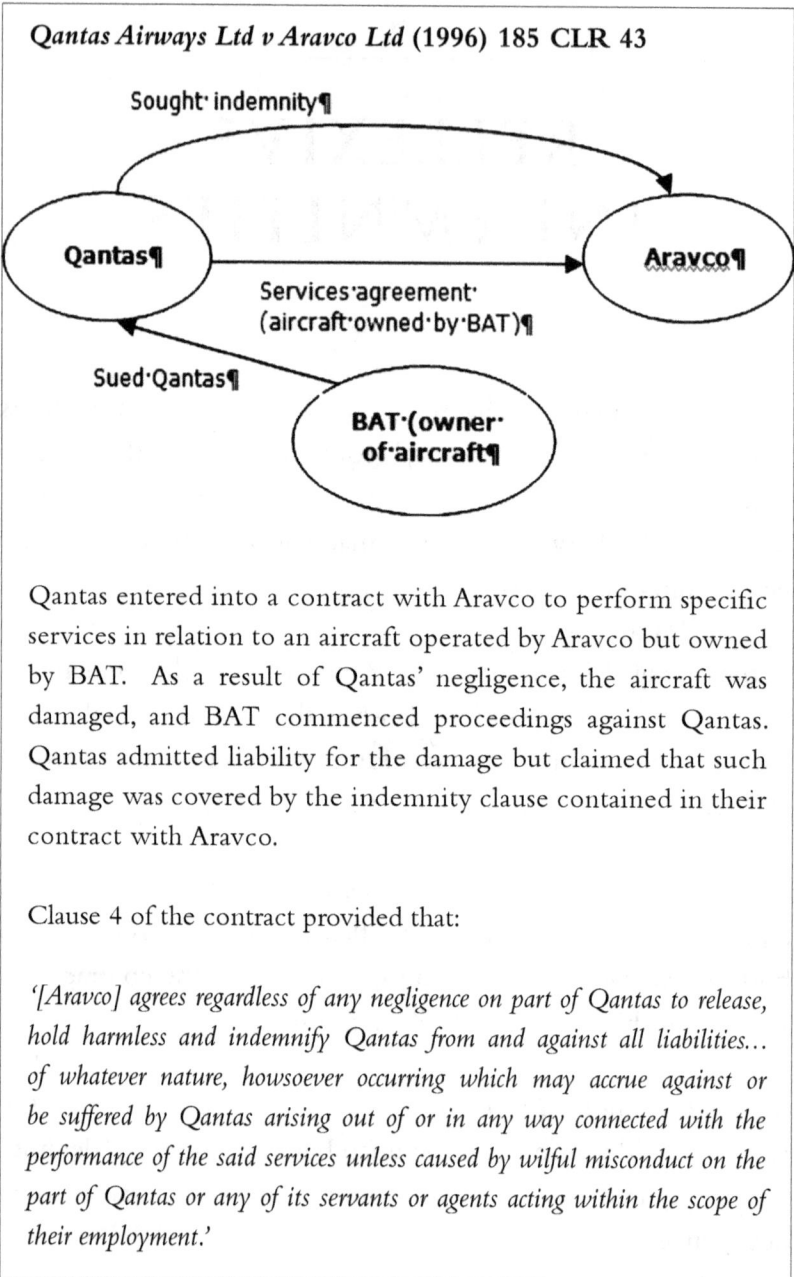

Qantas Airways Ltd v Aravco Ltd (1996) 185 CLR 43

Sought indemnity

Qantas

Services agreement
(aircraft owned by BAT)

Aravco

Sued Qantas

BAT (owner
of aircraft

Qantas entered into a contract with Aravco to perform specific services in relation to an aircraft operated by Aravco but owned by BAT. As a result of Qantas' negligence, the aircraft was damaged, and BAT commenced proceedings against Qantas. Qantas admitted liability for the damage but claimed that such damage was covered by the indemnity clause contained in their contract with Aravco.

Clause 4 of the contract provided that:

'[Aravco] agrees regardless of any negligence on part of Qantas to release, hold harmless and indemnify Qantas from and against all liabilities... of whatever nature, howsoever occurring which may accrue against or be suffered by Qantas arising out of or in any way connected with the performance of the said services unless caused by wilful misconduct on the part of Qantas or any of its servants or agents acting within the scope of their employment.'

The Court found that this clause required Aravco to indemnify Qantas for its own negligence.

Interestingly, the agreement between Qantas and Aravco was a consumer contract under the *Trade Practices Act 1974* (**TPA**) (now *Competition and Consumer Act 2010* (Cth)), as the services rendered by Qantas were valued at less than $40,000. As a result, there was an implied term in the contract between Aravco and Qantas that Qantas render its services with due care and skill (section 74 TPA). While not alleging a breach of section 74 TPA, Aravco argued that section 68 TPA, which makes void any term that attempts to exclude, restrict or modify an implied condition or warranty, operated to void Aravco's indemnity.

While Qantas did indeed breach the implied warranty of due care imposed by section 74 TPA, the Court held that the breach had no effect on the indemnification agreement. Aravco could not make a claim under section 74 unless it actually sued Qantas for breach of that warranty, which it did not.

The court held that the damages flowing from the breach of the warranty would likely have included the amount for which it was liable to reimburse Qantas under the indemnity clause – but Aravco's failure to plead the breach of warranty meant this outcome could not eventuate.

The following two cases are examples where the relevant indemnity clauses were **not** sufficient to apply 'reflexively'.

Ellington v Heinrich Constructions Pty Ltd & Ors [2005] QCA 475

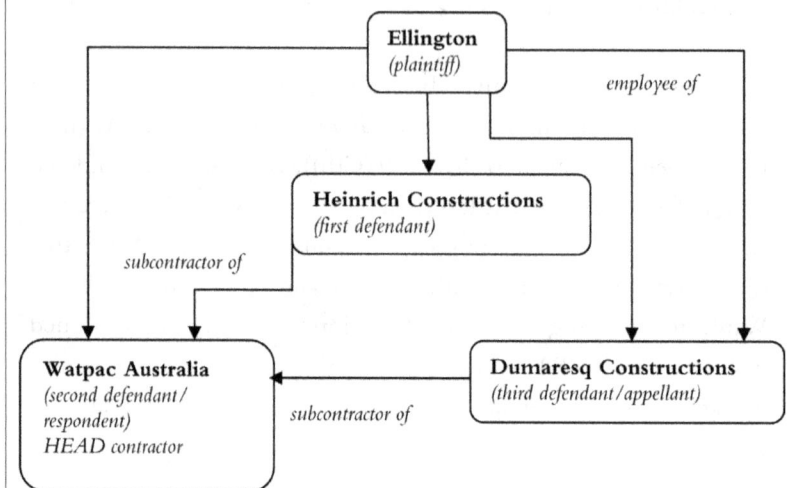

Ellington was employed as a steel fixer with Dumaresq, and was injured during the course of his employment. Ellington was assisting others in positioning a steel beam when he fell from the formwork some four metres onto the ground.

Ellington brought a claim against each of his employer (Dumaresq), the head contractor for the site (Watpac) and another subcontractor of Watpac's (Heinrich). The court found no liability on the part of Heinrich. The court found that both Watpac and Dumaresq had been negligent, and found Watpac was liable for two–thirds of Ellington's claim, and Dumaresq was liable for one–third of Ellington's claim.

Watpac sought to enforce an indemnity in its favour against Dumaresq, as follows:

'[Dumaresq] shall not commit any act of trespass or commit any nuisance or be guilty of any negligence **and shall effectually protect and hereby**

18

indemnifies [Watpac] and [Watpac's] employees against all loss, damage, injury or liability whatsoever that may occur in respect of the Works or through the execution of the Works and in case of any such loss, damage, injury or liability occurring [Dumaresq] shall make full compensation and shall make good all such loss, damage, injury or liability and if [Watpac] is required to pay any damages for such loss, damage, injury or liability the amount of such damages may together with all costs which [Watpac] may have incurred in defending or settling the claim for such damages may be deducted from any monies due or becoming due to [Dumaresq] under this Contract...'

AT TRIAL

Watpac argued that this indemnity applied to protect Watpac against both Dumaresq's negligence, and its own. In deciding that the indemnity did not apply to Watpac's negligence, the trial judge relied on the case of *Canberra Formwork Pty Ltd v Civil & Civic Ltd* (1982) 41 ACTR 1, which contained a very similarly worded provision, which omitted only the word 'whatsoever', and where the Court determined that the indemnity did not apply reflexively.

The trial judge stated (at 74]):

'Unless the clause is construed in this way, the subcontractor would be liable for losses sustained by the builder as a result of its negligence, its breaches of the head contract or breaches of statutory duty. It may even be arguable that the subcontractor would be liable for damages sustained by the builder as a result of its own deliberate wrongdoing. The parties, of course, may make such a contract if they wish, but in ascertaining the parties' intention, it is appropriate to have particular regard to textual indications that no such consequences were intended.

The fact that the subject provisions were agreed to by the parties well after the reported decision in Canberra Formwork Pty Ltd support the conclusion I have reached.'

However, another clause in the subcontracting agreement also required Dumaresq to take out insurance on behalf of itself and Watpac. The trial judge found that, had the insurance been taken out, Watpac would have been insured against Ellington's claim. The trial judge found that Dumaresq had breached its obligation to take out this insurance, and so was liable in any event to compensate Watpac for its two-thirds liability.

ON APPEAL

On appeal, Dumaresq argued that Watpac would not have been insured in the circumstances under the relevant insurance policy, had Dumaresq taken it out. Watpac again tried to argue that the indemnity applied in its favour in circumstances where Dumaresq had been negligent.

The appeal court affirmed the trial judge's finding that the indemnity clause did not protect Watpac where the loss was caused by Watpac's own negligence.

However, while Dumaresq was not successful in its argument that the insurance policy, if taken out, would not have insured Watpac in the circumstances, the decision was ultimately overturned, and Watpac ordered to pay Ellington its two-thirds damages, because no specified insurance amount was stated in the Schedule to the subcontracting agreement!

As a result, Dumaresq's promise to take out insurance was void because an essential term was uncertain. Dumaresq ultimately secured a victory through an argument discovered after judgment.

In the case of *Westina Corporation v BGC Contracting* [2009] WASCA 213, the Court found the relevant indemnity clause insufficient to apply reflexively despite the broad wording. ***Westina Corporation v BGC Contracting* [2009] WASCA 213**

indemnity owed to BGC under the Hire Agreement?

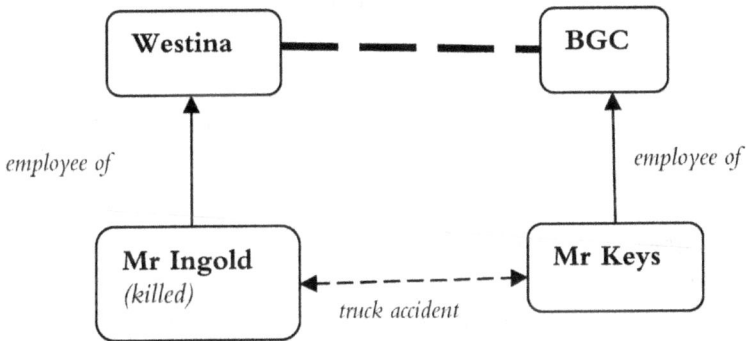

Westina owned a prime mover truck (**Jamieson truck**). Westina and BGC entered into an agreement under which BGC hired from Westina both the Jamieson truck and a licensed operator named Mr Ingold, who was an employee of Westina.

Mr Ingold was driving the Jamieson truck when it collided with another prime mover, which was owned by BGC and driven by one of BGC's employees. This collision, caused by BGC's employee, resulted in the death of Mr Ingold.

Westina commenced proceedings against BGC for the loss of the Jamieson truck and associated equipment.

BGC sought to rely on clause 9(e) of the Hire Agreement which stated:

'*Where the Plant is hired on a **Wet Hire** basis, the Supplier shall:... Bear the risk of loss in the hiring of the Plant and must defend, indemnify and hold BGC harmless against any injury, death, claim or other loss arising from the hiring of the Plant.*'

The main issue in this case was whether the clause acted as a 'reflexive indemnity clause', which would require Westina to indemnify BGC against BGC's own negligence. The trial judge held that it was; that BGC and Mr Keys were entitled to an indemnity from Westina on the basis of the above indemnity clause. However, Westina's appeal was successful and Westina was found to owe **no indemnity** to BGC and Mr Keys.

On appeal, the Court held that where there is doubt as to the construction of an indemnity clause, the issue must be resolved in favour of the indemnifier, which in this case was Westina.

Buss JA stated at [48]–[49]:

'*The construction of a written contract is concerned with ascertaining what a reasonable person would have understood the parties to mean. Consideration should ordinarily be given not only to the language of the document, but also to the surrounding circumstances known to the parties, and the apparent purpose and object of the transaction....*

Where, however, the written contract is a contract of guarantee or indemnity, a doubt as to the construction of a provision in the contract must be resolved in favour of the guarantor or indemnifier. See Andar Transport Pty Ltd v Brambles Ltd [2004] HCA 28....'

At [61], Buss JA then stated:

'*[The indemnity clause] does not expressly state whether the indemnity extends, without limit, to any future event, certain or uncertain, in connection with the Jamieson Truck and three trailers which occasions loss to BGC, irrespective of the identity of the person or entity whose act or omission caused the event and the connected loss, and irrespective of the nature and character of the conduct in question (for example, whether the act or omission was negligent or a breach of duty). There is doubt or uncertainty, in my opinion, as to whether the indemnity should be characterised as a 'reflexive indemnity'; that is, whether the indemnity was intended by Westina and BGC to apply to a liability which arises, as between them, from BGC's own default (in particular, its breach of duty under the law of negligence).*'

The Court then considered that fact that the indemnity only related to 'wet hires', as distinct from a 'dry hire'. A wet hire involves the hire of plant with an operator, where a dry hire involves the hire of plant without an operator. Therefore, the court said (at [68]−[69]):

'*The indemnity...must therefore be construed in the context that the Plant...is to be operated by the Supplier's (Westina's) employee, not BGC's employee. The evident intention of the parties was to protect BGC from any liabilities it may incur to third parties (that is, to persons or entities other than Westina) as a result of any injury, death, claim or other loss arising from the hiring of the Plant, in circumstances where those liabilities will invariable be incurred as a result of some negligent act or omission by Westina or its employee as the operator of the Plant. The confinement [in the indemnity] to wet hires suggests it was not intended that the [indemnity] should operate as a reflexive indemnity.*

In my opinion, the doubt or uncertainty attending the proper constructions of the [clause] is not resolved favourably to BGC...'

In *Samways v WorkCover Queensland & Ors* [2010] QSC 12, the indemnity clause was drafted in broad terms, but was still sufficient to require a head contractor to indemnify a subcontractor for the subcontractors' own negligence.

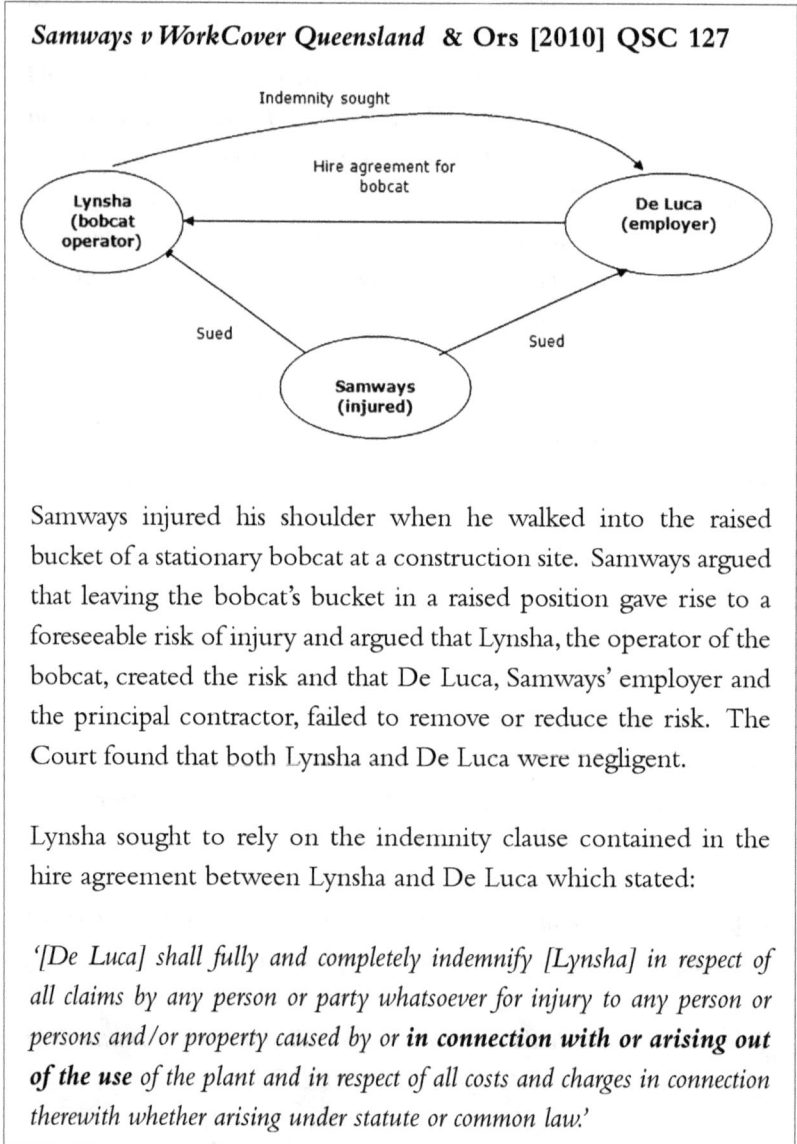

Samways v WorkCover Queensland & Ors [2010] QSC 127

Samways injured his shoulder when he walked into the raised bucket of a stationary bobcat at a construction site. Samways argued that leaving the bobcat's bucket in a raised position gave rise to a foreseeable risk of injury and argued that Lynsha, the operator of the bobcat, created the risk and that De Luca, Samways' employer and the principal contractor, failed to remove or reduce the risk. The Court found that both Lynsha and De Luca were negligent.

Lynsha sought to rely on the indemnity clause contained in the hire agreement between Lynsha and De Luca which stated:

*'[De Luca] shall fully and completely indemnify [Lynsha] in respect of all claims by any person or party whatsoever for injury to any person or persons and/or property caused by or **in connection with or arising out of the use** of the plant and in respect of all costs and charges in connection therewith whether arising under statute or common law.'*

The Supreme Court held that the terms 'in connection with' and 'arising out of' have wide meanings. Even though the bobcat was not in operation at the time of the accident, the deployment of the bobcat to the site constituted 'use' for the purposes of the hire agreement and indemnity clause.

The court approved the judicial reasoning in *Andar* that any doubt as to the construction of an indemnity clause should be resolved in favour of the indemnifier, but also noted at [67] that *'...a court has no mandate to rewrite a provision to avoid what it retrospectively perceives as commercial unfairness or lack of balance'*.

The Court also looked at the context of the entire clause and held that the commercial and contractual context of the clause did not make it improbable that Lynsha would seek to be indemnified by its own negligence. Lynsha was therefore entitled to a full indemnity from De Luca.

SUBROGATION

An interesting issue to consider in respect of contractual indemnities is the extent to which the doctrine of subrogation may be used.

It is generally accepted that, subject to statute or contrary terms in the contract, a mere promise to indemnify a party does not give the indemnifying party an obligation to defend a claim against the indemnified party. Nor does the indemnifying party have a general right to defend the third party claim.[6] It is important to expressly include such a right to be able to do this to prevent

---

6   Ibid

being liable for the outcome, which will often be a settlement if left to the control of the indemnified.

However, once an indemnifier has paid out an indemnified party's claim, the doctrine of subrogation may apply, and the indemnifier may have an equitable right to step into the shoes of the indemnified and pursue the party that caused the loss.

Importantly, an indemnifier who claims a right of subrogation must have first paid the indemnified under the indemnity.

EXCLUSIVE REMEDY

Academic consideration in Australia suggests that if parties to an agreement agree to an indemnity with respect to breach, then any compensation resulting from a breach will, as a matter of construction, be determined by reference to the indemnity.[7] That is, it is an exclusive remedy.

So if obtaining the benefit of an indemnity, depending on the terms, clarification is needed that this is an additional right under the agreement to preserve the ability to claim damages calculated by general law principles.

---

[7] 'Indemnities against breach', Professor John Carter, Contractual Indemnities Conference, Sydney, 30 July 2010

CIVIL LIABILITY LEGISLATION

Various pieces of legislation were enacted following difficulties in people obtaining insurance for public events in the late 1990s and early 2000s (e.g. *Civil Liability Act 2003 (Qld), Pt 2*).

This so−called Civil Liability legislation introduced the notion of proportionate liability, which serves to limit a wrongdoer's liability to that proportion of the loss claimed that a court considers just having regard to the particular wrongdoer's responsibility for that loss. That is, if more than one person is responsible for the loss, the legislation limits the ability of the aggrieved party to sue the wrongdoer with the deepest pockets for the full amount.

One would not expect this regime to apply to an allocation of risk between parties to a commercial contract. However, two areas of uncertainty have been raised.[8]

The first is whether or not the regime applies to a strict contractual claim (e.g. a claim against a contracting party based on a breach of an obligation or warranty other than to take reasonable care if the breach was caused by the fault of a third party who may also be sued in negligence). This has not been settled by the courts,

---

[8] 'Indemnities and the Civil Liabilities Legislation', Professor Barbara McDonald, Contractual Indemnities Conference, Sydney, 30 July 2010

but academic consideration is that the better view is that the legislation was not intended to apply to such situations.[9]

The second concern is about whether or not the contractual allocation of risk between joint wrongdoers is effective. Specifically, each Act provides that a defendant is not required to 'indemnify' another wrongdoer. Academic consideration of the legislation again suggests that these words cannot be given a literal meaning. Instead these words should be considered as only restricting the power of a court to order an indemnity as part of an apportionment between defendants (as no such apportionment would be necessary given the restriction on the amount recoverable).[10]

The alternative view would be that joint wrongdoers cannot apportion liability between themselves through indemnities except in jurisdictions in which contracting out of the regime is permitted.

Practically, at least in Queensland, there appears to be little to be done when drafting indemnities. Until these concerns are clarified through the Courts you should consider the application of the Civil Liability legislation further should you be faced with a claim in circumstances in which there are multiple wrongdoers and risk has been allocated by way of a contractual indemnity.

---

[9] B McDonald and JW Carter, 'The Lottery of Contractual Risk Allocation and Proportionate Liability' (2009) 26 JCL 1

[10] 'Indemnities and the Civil Liabilities Legislation', Professor Barbara McDonald, Contractual Indemnities Conference, Sydney, 30 July 2010

6

DRAFTING AND NEGOTIATING INDEMNITIES

WHAT TO LOOK FOR AS THE INDEMNIFIER

The issue of indemnity is a very serious one and as a rule should be avoided where possible. Having said this, in certain transactions an indemnity may be expected with respect to certain events, and may be commercially required in order to do business. For example, as contemplated by paragraph 1.4 above, it is usual in negotiated intellectual property licences to indemnify the licensee against some if not all claims by a third party that the exercise of the rights being licensed by the licensee infringes their intellectual property rights.

- As with exclusions and warranties, not all indemnities are the same, and there is still much scope for negotiation when granting an indemnity. The approach should include:
- limiting the indemnity to 'direct loss' only;
- avoiding broad phrases such as 'in connection with' and replacing them with words such as 'caused solely by' or similar;
- resisting reference to the other party's negligence (and perhaps expressly exclude liability in connection with it);
- excluding loss to the extent contributed to by the other party;

- limiting liability to final judgments or some other third party liability rather than any loss or damage;
- excluding legal fees, or clarifying they are on a party–party basis;
- clarifying that the indemnity is subject to any exclusions or limitations of liability contained in the agreement; and
- requiring the indemnified party to mitigate its loss.

There may also be other mechanisms in certain areas of the law that experienced lawyers should be asked about.

A system should be developed in regards to notification of claims and the process to defend them. It is often in the best interest of parties to be able to control proceedings to reduce the risk of a court making a finding that may be adverse to business outside the relationship in question.

WHAT TO LOOK FOR AS THE INDEMNIFIED

Similarly, the indemnified must:

- be aware of what indemnities are 'usual' for the class of document being negotiated;
- use broad words when connecting the indemnity with the events being indemnified against (e.g. 'in connection with' rather than 'due to' or 'caused by');
- be specific in relation to losses most concerned about;
- be specific about particular events most concerned about;
- consider whether or they can sue for the breach independently of the indemnity in relation to the area of concern (i.e. how will the risk profile change if the indemnity is not granted?);
- remember that third party claims are usually but not necessarily the most important;

- clarify that the indemnities are not subject to any applicable limitation or exclusion of liability under the agreement;
- clarify they do not have to incur any expense or make payment before making a claim under an indemnity (there have been cases in which claims have failed as the indemnified party has not yet incurred the loss);
- try to refer to legal fees expressly as they are often a major expense; and
- don't forget privity of contract – it is of no use indemnifying people who are not party to the agreement unless they come within one of the limited exceptions to the rule of privity.

Remember of course that, as with everything being negotiated, one can elect to accept the risk and proceed with the contract to get the benefit of the contract (practical if not legal). For example, a small purchaser of a Microsoft Office licence may not get much of an indemnity from Microsoft, if any, but if he or she wishes to use Office without infringing Microsoft's IP then the risk of infringing a third party's IP without the benefit of an indemnity may well be a risk he or she is prepared to take.

EXAMPLE INDEMNITY CLAUSES

As the indemnified:

Indemnity

The Supplier indemnifies the Customer from and against, all loss or damage incurred or suffered by the Customer however caused in connection with:

- *any breach of this deed by the Supplier;*
- *any claim by the Supplier against the Customer in connection with this deed;*
- *the enforcement of the Customer's rights in connection with any alleged or actual breach of this deed by the Supplier;*
- *any claim or allegation that the Deliverables, exercise of the rights contemplated by clause [x] or the provision of the Services infringes the Intellectual Property Rights or other rights of any third party;*
- *personal injury or death of any person (including any employee of the Supplier) at premises owned or occupied by the Customer or in connection with the provision of the Services; or*
- *any act or omission of the Supplier, its officers, employees or agents.*

As the indemnifier:

'Indemnity

- *Subject to clause (c) and the Customer complying with clause (b), the Supplier indemnifies the Customer from any loss or damage caused by claim by a third party that use of the Software by the Customer infringes the intellectual property rights of a third party.*
- *If the Customer becomes aware of a third party claim contemplated by clause (a) the Customer must:*

   (i) *immediately notify Supplier and provide Supplier with all information available to the Customer;*
   (ii) *use its best endeavours to mitigate the loss suffered by the Customer;*

(iii) *consent to Supplier conducting the defence or settling the claim (as determined in Supplier's discretion);*

(iv) *provide any assistance requested by Supplier; and*

(v) *not make any statement or admission in relation to the claim without Supplier's prior consent.*

- *The Supplier is not liable under the indemnity in clause (a) to the extent that the loss or damage was caused or contributed to by any act or omission of the Customer.'*

7

WHY EXCLUSION CLAUSES ARE IMPORTANT

In general, exclusion clauses provide defences to a claim for breach of contract, and their effect will depend on both the construction of the contract as a whole, and the particular wording of the exclusion clause.

While most commercial agreements contain exclusions of liability, it is imperative careful consideration is given to the nature and wording of the obligations and the warranties provided. If at all possible, it is far preferable to not breach an agreement than to mount a defence for a claim of damages for loss caused by that breach.

If an agreement is silent on liability then each party's liability under the agreement is said to be unlimited, subject to the usual common law requirement that the damage be caused by the breach and not be too remote. The general rule for the assessment of damages for breach of an agreement is to place the non–breaching parties in the position they would had been in had the breaching party performed its obligations. While this may be good news for a customer or purchaser, it may not seem like such a great deal to the supplier of a $50 software package being used to control an assembly line.

To prevent a situation that deprives a party an ability to seek damages, scrutinising broadly drafted exclusion clauses is required.

EXAMPLES

In general, there are three types of exclusion clauses, being exclusion clauses that:

- completely exclude liability for particular conduct – for example:

  'The Supplier is not liable for any loss or damage suffered by the Customer in connection with this agreement whether caused by negligence or otherwise.'

- limit or restrict liability for particular conduct – for example:

  'Any liability of the Supplier for any loss or damage, whether caused by negligence or otherwise, suffered by the Customer in connection with this agreement is limited to the fees paid by the Customer to the Supplier under this agreement in the 12 months prior to the date of the first loss or damage suffered

- qualify rights and remedies for breach of contract – for example:

  'Any claim by the Customer against the Supplier for loss or damage, whether caused by negligence or otherwise, suffered by the Customer in connection with a defective Product must be made within 30 days of the date that the Customer discovers, or ought reasonably to have discovered the defect.'

8

HOW EXCLUSION CLAUSES ARE INTERPRETED

Traditionally courts have gone out of their way to read down exclusion clauses. However, with the advent of consumer protection legislation such as *Trade Practices Act 1974* (Cth) (now the *Competition and Consumer Act 2010* (Cth)), there appears to have been a move towards interpreting exclusion clauses in the same way other clauses are interpreted, especially between commercial entities.

The leading United Kingdom case of *Photo Production Ltd v Securicor Transport Ltd* [1980] AC 827 at 843 demonstrates this move towards a more commercial approach to construing exclusion clauses.

Photo Production Ltd v Securicor Transport Ltd

In this case, Securicor was engaged by Photo Production to provide a night patrol service for Photo Production's factory. Securicor's standard form of contract had a condition which stated:

'*Under no circumstances shall [Securicor] be responsible for any injurious act or default by any employee of the company unless such act or default*

---

could have been foreseen and avoided by the exercise of due diligence of the part of [Securicor] as his employer...'

While on patrol, an employee of Securicor lit a fire which ended up burning the factory down (the employee only meant to start a small fire but it later got out of control). The employee who started the fire had a good work record, had provided satisfactory references to Securicor and had been employed by Securicor for approximately four months when the incident occurred.

The Court of Appeal found the exclusion clause to be invalid, as Securicor had committed a 'fundamental breach' of the agreement.

On appeal to the House of Lords, the court agreed that the breach of contract caused an event that rendered further performance of the contract impossible (i.e. destruction of the factory), and so 'it is not an unnatural use of the ordinary language to described it as a "fundamental breach"'.

However, despite the fundamental breach, the court said that '*...this does not entitle the court to reject the exclusion clause, however unreasonable the court itself may think it is, if the words are clear and fairly susceptible of one meaning only.'* The court applied a rule of construction and found the exclusion clause effective.

Lord Diplock said (at 851):

'[I]n the absence of the exclusion clause...a primary obligation of Securicor under the contract, which would be implied by law, would be an absolute obligation to procure that the visits by the night patrol to the factory were conducted by natural persons who would exercise reasonable skill and care for the safety of the factory. That primary obligation is modified by the exclusion clause. Securicor's obligation to do this is not to be absolute, but is

limited to exercising due diligence in its capacity as employer of the natural persons by whom the visits are conducted, and to procure that those persons shall exercise reasonable skill and care for the safety of the factory.'

Lord Diplock said further (at 851):

'In commercial contracts negotiated between business-men capable of looking after their own interests and of deciding how risks inherent in the performance of various kinds of contract can be most economically borne (generally by insurance), it is, in my view, wrong to place a strained construction upon words in an exclusion clause which are clear and fairly susceptible of one meaning only even after due allowance has been made for the presumption in favour of the implied primary and secondary obligations.'

Lord Wilberforce said (at 843):

'[I]n commercial matters generally, when the parties are not of unequal bargaining power, and when risks are normally borne by insurance, not only is the case for judicial intervention undemonstrated, but there is everything to be said ... for leaving the parties free to apportion the risks as they think fit and for respecting their decisions.'

The High Court decision of *Darlington Futures Ltd v Delco Australia Pty Ltd* (1986) 161 CLR 500 approved the statements made by Lord Wilberforce and Lord Diplock in *Photo Production*, as stated above, and is the leading Australian case on exclusion clauses.

Darlington Futures Ltd v Delco Australia Pty Ltd

In this case, Darlington was engaged by Delco to engage on Delco's behalf in 'tax straddles', a form of commodities futures dealings. The parties had executed a contract which contained a

number of questions. One question was 'Do you wish this account
to be traded at the discretion of Darlington Futures Ltd?' The
answer was 'No'. In breach of Delco's instructions, Darlington
engaged in certain unauthorised trading, which resulted in a loss
to Delco of around $280,000. The court found that Darlington's
unauthorised trading was not mere negligent performance of
Delco's instructions, but went 'beyond the ambit of the authority'
given by Delco to Darlington.

Relevantly, clause 6 of the agreement provided:

'...[Delco]... acknowledges that [Darlington] will not be responsible for
any loss arising in any way out of any trading activity undertaking on
behalf of [Delco] whether pursuant to this Agreement or not...'.

Clause 7 of the agreement also provided:

'...Any liability on [Darlington's] part or on the part of its servants
or agents for damages for or in respect of any claim arising out of or in
connection with the relationship established by this Agreement or any
conduct under it or any orders or instructions given to [Darlington] by
[Delco]... shall not in any event (and whether or not such liability results
from or involves negligence) exceed one hundred dollars.'

The court held (at 510) that:

'...[T]he interpretation of an exclusion clause is to be determined by
construing the clause according to its natural and ordinary meaning, read in
the light of the contract as a whole, thereby giving due weight to the context
in which the clause appears including the nature and object of the contract,
and, where appropriate, construing the clause contra proferentem in case of
ambiguity...

The court went on to say, in relation to limitation of liability clauses, that:

[T]he same principle applies to the construction of limitation clauses.... [A] limitation clause may be so severe in its operation as to make its effect virtually indistinguishable from that of an exclusion clause. And the principle, in the form in which we have expressed it, does no more than express the general approach to the interpretation of contracts and it is of sufficient generality to accommodate the different considerations that may arise in the interpretation of a wide variety of exclusion and limitation clauses in formal commercial contracts between business people where no question of the reasonableness or fairness of the clause arises.'

In relation to clause 6 of the Agreement, the court found that Darlington's liability was not excluded as:

'...it can scarcely be supposed that the parties intended to exclude liability on the part of [Darlington] for losses arising from trading activity it which it presumed to engage on behalf of [Delco] when [Darlington] had no authority to do so.'

In relation to clause 7, the court found that Darlington's liability was excluded:

'...is expressed to comprehend claims arising out of or in connection with the relationship established by the agreement. A claim in respect of an unauthorised transaction may none the less have a connection, indeed a substantial connection, with the relationship of broker and client established by the agreement.'

The court could not discern any basis on which clause 7 could be construed as not applying to the claim, and so the clause operated to limit Darlington's liability to $100 in respect of each of unauthorised transaction.

In summary, *Darlington* is authority for the proposition that exclusion clauses must be given their natural and ordinary meaning, construed in light of the contract as a whole, with any ambiguity resolved *contra proferentem* (i.e. against the party relying on the exclusion clause).

There are many manifestations to the *Darlington* proposition that one needs to construe the exclusion clause in light of the contract as a whole. The effect is that, in some circumstances (always depending on the construction of the particular exclusion clause), certain breaches may fall outside the scope of the exclusion clause, for example where the breach:

- is a breach of a fundamental or essential term;
- is wilful in character;
- occurs by the supply of a subject matter which is completely different from that contracted for;
- appears to defeat what may reasonably be described as the main purpose of the contract; or
- takes the performance of the party alleged to be in breach outside the 'four corners' of the contract.

It is important to remember, however, that the function of an exclusion clause will always be a question of construction, and there is no rule of law that an exclusion clause can never exclude liability for breaches such as fundamental or wilful breaches if the intention of the parties is clear.

The case of *Lime Telecom Pty Ltd v Powertel Ltd* [No 1] [2008] NSWSC 324 is a recent decision which demonstrates the courts' reluctance to give effect to exclusion clauses (even broadly drafted ones) in the face of serious breaches such as repudiatory conduct.

Lime Telecom Pty Ltd v Powertel Ltd

In this case, PowerTel supplied telecommunications services to Lime. Through the course of the relationship (nearly 3 years) Lime rarely complied with its monthly payment regime. At the end of the relationship, PowerTel alleged that it sent a notice of a form permitted by the agreement between the parties demanding payment. PowerTel alleged that Lime failed to comply with the notice, and so PowerTel purported to terminate all the agreements between Lime and itself.

Lime contended that it never received the notice demanding payment. The court favoured Lime's evidence. As a result, the court found that PowerTel had wrongfully terminated (i.e. repudiated) the relevant contract.

Relevantly, the 'Limitation of Liability' clause under the agreement stated as follows:

'14.4 Except as otherwise expressly provided in this Agreement... and to the extent permitted by law, a party has no liability to the other party in connection with this Agreement for or in respect of any consequential loss, indirect loss, loss of profits of any kind, loss or corruption of data, interruption to business, loss of customers or customer losses, loss or revenue and economic loss of any kind, whether in contract, negligence or any other tort under any statute or otherwise.'

PowerTel sought to rely on this clause 14.4 to exclude their liability for breach of contract.

McDouglas J held that:

'...[W]hen one looks at cl 15 as a whole and in context, one could not say, to adapt the wording of the court in Darlington Futures at 511, that the parties intended to exclude liability on the part of PowerTel for losses arising from activities outside the scope of performance (or non-performance or malperformance) of the contract. When one looks at cl 14.4, it seems to me clearly enough to be aimed at any activity that has the effect of reducing the services that PowerTel was obliged to supply, or reducing the ambit of those services, or depriving Lime of the benefit of those services. I accept that it may be said that a repudiation of the agreements would have the effect of depriving Lime of the benefit of them. However, the effect of such a construction is to say that, notwithstanding the very carefully worded contractual scheme that is to be found in the more than 60 pages of the standard terms, the parties nonetheless contemplated that PowerTel could, at its option, wrongfully and without any reason whatsoever decide not to provide or perform any further service and escape scot free.'

FOUR CORNERS RULE

While again a question of construction, the 'four corners' rule is an often quoted rule, and so is worth considering. The most famous formulation is that of Lord Justice Scrutton in *Gibaud v Great Eastern Railway Co* [1921] 2 KB 426 at 435:

'The principle is well known ... that if you undertake to do a thing in a certain way, or to keep a thing in a certain place, with certain conditions protecting it, and have broken the contract by not doing the thing contracted for in the way contracted for, or not keeping the article in the place in which you have contracted to keep it, you cannot rely on the conditions which were only intended to protect you if you carried out the contract in the way in which you had contracted to do it.'

43

The key Australia case is *Sydney Corp v West* (1965) 114 CLR 481.

Sydney Corp v West

In this case, West parked his car in a Sydney City Council car park. The ticket he received included 'Parking Conditions', which stated, relevantly, that:

'The Council does not accept any responsibility for the loss or damage to any vehicle or for loss of or damage to any article or thing in or upon any vehicle or for any injury to any person however such loss, damage or injury may arise or be caused.'

The Parking Conditions also stated that the ticket had to be presented before the vehicle was taken from the car park. The court heard and accepted evidence that the car park attendant for Sydney Corp had delivered West's vehicle to another person ('Robinson') without any authorisation from West and notwithstanding Robinson's inability to produce a parking ticket. In fact, a duplicate ticket was issued to Robinson.

The High Court held that Sydney Corp was unable to rely on the exclusion clause because the clause had no application where Sydney Corp had been negligent and dealt with West's car in a way that was neither authorised nor permitted by the contract.

Barwick CJ and Taylor CJ said (at 489) that:

'[T]he act of the attendant in permitting 'Robinson' to proceed after handing over the duplicate ticket which he had obtained constituted an unauthorized delivery of possession by him to 'Robinson' and not a mere act of negligence in relation to some act authorized by the contract of bailment.'

Practically, the 'rules' regarding exclusion clauses should not change how they are approached. However, if a party is seeking to rely on an exclusion clause to avoid liability, the rules should be considered as they may be used to argue that the exclusion clause was never intended to apply to the particular breach due to its wilful or serious nature.

NEGLIGENCE

An exclusion clause may exclude or limit any form of liability, unless the liability is prohibited by public policy or statute. This includes liability for torts, such as negligence, and in fact it is common to see clauses in service contracts that attempt to exclude or limit liability for negligence.

Traditionally, courts have taken a strict approach to the exclusion of liability for negligence. This is because negligence often results in property damage or personal injury (as opposed to pure economic loss), and so the court have usually said that the relevant exclusion clause must state a clear intention to exclude negligence. Interestingly, clauses purporting to exclude liability of 'any loss' have historically been treated as insufficient to exclude liability for negligence, but by contrast, the words 'whatever its cause' or 'howsoever caused' have been treated as sufficient.[11]

In more recent times, however, there has been a shift towards treating exclusions for negligence in the same way as other exclusion clauses (*Darlington*). Despite this trend, if seeking to exclude liability for negligence, out of an abundance of caution it

---

[11] *Commissioner for Railways (NSW) v Quinn* (1946) 72 CLR 345

is always best to do so expressly. This will remove any doubt on the question of construction.

LIABILITY CAPS

While there is no case law on point, it may be preferable as a supplier to limit liability to a small cap (e.g. $100) rather than to completely exclude liability. While comments made in *Darlington* suggest that clauses seeking to limit liability should be construed the same as any other clauses seeking to exclude liability, the case did not deal with complete exclusions of liability, and so the position is unclear.

9

CONSEQUENTIAL LOSS

TRADITIONAL VIEW

Suppliers spend much time arguing for liability for 'consequential loss' to be excluded from their supply contracts. The meaning of this phrase is not clear under Australian law – the High Court has not considered it.

However, there has been judicial support for the proposition that 'consequential loss', along with the term 'indirect loss', means loss recoverable under the so called 'second limb' of *Hadley v Baxendale* (1854) 9 Ex 341. Damages under the first limb of the rule in *Hadley v Baxendale* are sometimes described as 'direct loss' and those contemplated by the second limb are sometimes described as 'indirect loss'.

The 'two limbs' formulation in *Hadley v Baxendale* is the basic rule governing the law of remoteness of damage in contract.

Hadley v Baxendale

In this case, Hadley owned a milling business. As a crankshaft of a steam engine at Hadley's mill had broken, Hadley engaged Baxendale to deliver the crankshaft to engineers for repair by a certain date. Baxendale failed to deliver the crankshaft on time, causing Hadley to lose business. Hadley sued Baxendale for these lost profits.

The court did not award Hadley these lost profits as Hadley had failed to mention his special circumstances in advance.

The two limbs stated by Alderson B (at 354):

'Where two parties have made a contract which one of them has broken, the damages which the other party ought to receive in respect of such breach of contract should be:

1. *such as may fairly and reasonably be considered either arising naturally, i.e., according to the usual course of things, from such breach of contract itself; or*
2. *such as may reasonably be supposed to have been in the contemplation of both parties, at the time they had made the contract, as the probably result of the breach of it.'*

(numbering added)

The court went on to say that:

'Now, if the special circumstances under which the contract was actually made were communicated by the plaintiffs to the defendants, and thus known to both parties, the damages resulting from the breach of such a contract, which they would reasonably contemplate, would be the amount of injury which would ordinarily follow from a breach of contract under these special circumstances so known and communicated.'

Recent United Kingdom cases have supported the view that the term 'consequential loss' is equivalent to loss falling under the second limb in *Hadley v Baxendale*.

In *British Sugar Plc v NEI Power Projects Ltd* (1997) 87 BLR 45, the court found that damages could be recovered for those losses that 'flowed naturally and directly' from the breach, with the 'consequential loss' exclusion applying only '*...in relation to some other type of loss which did not flow so directly, for example, damage which might flow from special circumstances and come within the second limb of Hadley v Baxendale*'.

In *Frank Davies Pty Ltd v Container Haulage Group Pty Ltd* (1989) 98 FLR 289, the relevant exclusion clause excluded liability for 'special or consequential damage of any nature whatsoever or howsoever caused'. The court held that the term 'consequential loss' was of the same kind as the term 'special', and so limited the exclusion to those losses properly within the second limb of *Hadley v Baxendale*.

Interpreting consequential loss as meaning loss contemplated by the second limb of *Hadley v Baxendale* has meant that certain exclusion clauses have been read down where the term consequential loss is identified as 'including' other types of losses – e.g. 'consequential loss including loss of profits'. These types of clauses have often been read down by the courts as referring only to losses that fall within the second limb of *Hadley v Baxendale*.

For example, in the United Kingdom case of *Pegler Ltd v Wang (UK) Ltd (No 1)* [2000] CLR 218, the relevant exclusion clause read:

> '*Wang shall not in any event be liable for any indirect, special or consequential loss, howsoever caused (including but not limited to loss of anticipated profits or data) in connection with or arising out of the supply, functioning or use of the Hardware, the Software or the Services.*'

49

In this case, the court held that the clause only excluded losses falling within the second limb of *Hadley v Baxendale*. The losses that were claimed included such losses as loss of sales and loss of opportunity to increase margins. As these losses were found to fall under the first limb of *Hadley v Baxendale*, they were recoverable.

AFTER PEERLESS

The Victorian Court of Appeal in the recent case of *Environmental Systems Pty Ltd v Peerless Holdings Pty Ltd* [2008] VSCA 26 (**Peerless**) has adopted a new approach to the construction of the term 'consequential loss'.

Environmental Systems Pty Ltd v Peerless Holdings Pty Ltd

In this case, Peerless bought a system from Environmental Systems for reducing odour emissions at Peerless' animal rendering plant. The system did not work as intended and was unable to deal with the odour satisfactorily.

The contract between the parties contained the following clause:

'*As a matter of policy, Environmental Systems does not accept liquidated damages or consequential loss…*'

Peerless claimed damages for:

- the cost of purchasing the system;
- the cost to it of its employees involved in attempting to make the system functional;
- the cost of dismantling and disposing of the system; and
- additional energy costs.

At first instance, Peerless succeeded in its claim. The trial judge held that the term 'consequential loss' referred to losses recoverable under the second limb of *Hadley v Baxendale*.

On appeal, the Victorian Court of Appeal held that the term 'consequential loss' should be given its ordinary and natural meaning and that the true distinction is between:

- normal loss, which is loss that every plaintiff in a like situation will suffer; and
- consequential loss, which is 'anything beyond the normal measure', such as profits lost and expenses incurred through breach.

As a result, the court found that the following losses were excluded as going beyond the normal measure (i.e. losses that not every plaintiff in a like situation would suffer):

- the cost to it of its employees involved in attempting to make the system functional; and
- additional energy costs.

This broadens the meaning of the term 'consequential loss' beyond its historically accepted meaning to include some losses falling within the first limb of *Hadley v Baxendale*.

For example, prior to *Peerless*, losses such as lost profits, increased production costs and expenses associated with removing a defective product may not have been excludable as 'consequential losses', as they may have arisen naturally from a breach of the contract itself (i.e. the first limb of *Hadley v Baxendale*). After *Peerless*, these sorts of losses could be interpreted as 'consequential losses'.

The decision in *Peerless* was not appealed to the High Court and it is uncertain what the High Court's view will be if or when it considers the issue.

In the meantime, best practice is to be specific about the kinds of loss that a provision will cover, and the kinds of loss which are excluded. The following sample clause provides an example of how this can be done:

> *The Supplier is not liable for any Consequential Loss whether caused by negligence or otherwise, suffered by the Customer in connection with this agreement.*
>
> *'Consequential Loss' in clause [x] means:*
>
> - *indirect loss;*
> - *consequential loss;*
> - *loss of bargain;*
> - *loss of revenues;*
> - *loss of profits; or*
> - *loss or damage in connection with claims against the Customer by third parties.*

Similarly, an example of a customer friendly clause would be:

> *'Neither party is liable for any Consequential Loss suffered by the other party that is caused by a breach of any warranty under this deed.*
>
> *'Consequential Loss' in clause [x] means any indirect loss recoverable at law which is:*
>
> - *loss caused by an error or defect in the new software;*
> - *loss of income or revenue; or*
> - *a loss of profits.*

10

AUSTRALIAN CONSUMER LAW

While commercial parties have significant freedom in deciding what terms to include in their contracts, there may be some limits to the exercise of a party's right to exclude or limit liability. For example, the new unfair contracts regime in the Australian Consumer Law (**ACL**) may operate to prevent a supplier of goods or services from relying on an exclusion clause where that clause is expressed in a standard form contract and is deemed to be 'unfair'.

The consumer guarantees under the ACL may also restrict a party's ability to exclude or limit liability for certain conduct. The consumer guarantees replace the old regime of implied warranties and conditions under the *Trade Practices Act 1974 (Cth)*.

Where the consumer guarantees applies, a supplier who purports to limit or exclude liability for breach of any guarantee (e.g. a guarantee that goods will be of 'acceptable quality') in circumstances where they are not permitted to do so may be misleading a consumer about their rights.

While it is not an offence per se to contravene a consumer guarantee provision, it is an offence for any person, in trade or commerce, to make false or misleading representations about goods or services (section 152 ACL). This includes making a false or misleading representation concerning the existence, exclusion or effect of the consumer guarantees (section 152(1)(m)).

The maximum civil penalty for providing false or misleading information is $1.1 million for a body corporate and $220,000 for an individual. Criminal penalties for the same amounts may also be imposed.

Where the consumer guarantees apply, the ACL may permit suppliers of goods or services to limit their liability in certain circumstances. Section 64A ACL provides that where goods are not of a kind ordinarily acquired for personal, domestic or household use or consumption, a term is not void under section 64 ACL by reason only that the term limits liability for failure to comply with a guarantee:

- in the case of goods – to replacement, repair or payment of the cost of replacing goods;
- in the case of services – to supplying the services again or payment of the cost of having the services supplied again.

Note that section 64A does not apply where the consumer establishes that it is not fair or reasonable for the supplier to rely on that term of the contract.

When attempting to exclude or limit liability in circumstances where the consumer guarantees may apply, great care needs to be taken, and the consumer's rights under the *Competition and Consumer Act* 2010 should be expressly referred to in your drafting. Here is an example clause that may assist to avoid misleading a consumer about their rights:

'Limitation of liability

- *Subject to clauses (b) and (c), any liability of the Supplier for any loss or damage whether caused by negligence or otherwise suffered by the Customer in connection with this agreement is limited to $100.*
- *Except as contemplated by clause (c), nothing in this agreement is intended to limit any rights of the Customer under the Competition and Consumer Act 2010 (Cth).*
- *If the Competition and Consumer Act 2010 (Cth) or any other legislation provides that there is a guarantee in relation to any good or service supplied by the Supplier in connection with this agreement and the Supplier's liability for failing to comply with that Vguarantee cannot be excluded but may be limited, then clause (a) does not apply to that liability and instead the Supplier's liability for such failure is limited to (at the Supplier's election):*

    (i) *in the case of a supply of goods, the Supplier replacing the goods or supplying equivalent goods, repairing the goods, paying the cost of replacing the goods or of acquiring equivalent goods, or paying the cost of having the goods repaired; or*

    (ii) *in the case of a supply of services, the Supplier supplying the services again or paying the cost of having the services supplied again.'*

11

PRACTICAL TIPS

When reviewing exclusion clauses the following needs to be considered:

- while the allocation of risk is a commercial issue, someone experienced in the area will have a feel for what is a good or acceptable position and what is a poor or unacceptable position. It is important to get a feel for the respective position of each party – how important the deal is and what a particular party can get away with. If a bargaining position justifies it, a party should not be shy in pursuing an aggressive risk profile or if the other party is not particularly sophisticated. Similarly, depending on this assessed position one may be forced to accept a poor risk profile to do the deal;

- contracting parties often try to effectively exclude all liability or limit it to a small amount. This needs to be carefully reviewed as a few words can remove the ability to sue for damages;

- if an agreement does not contain any limitation or exclusion of liability then liability can be said to be unlimited, which may be of concern depending on the nature of the agreement and the stated obligations under the agreement;

- when each party's liability is unlimited then it is often best not to raise the issue as any limitation or exclusion is likely to end up being for the benefit of both parties;

- often in supply contracts a commercial middle ground is to limit liability to a multiple of the fees payable over a 12 month period and to exclude certain categories of loss such as indirect and consequential–style losses;

- beware of limitations to fees paid as in many cases no fees will have been paid at the time when the risk is greatest (at the beginning of a project) – it is preferable to limit liability to the higher of a multiple of the fees expected to pay and the amount actually paid;

- for supplier clauses it is often the best policy to exclude a broad list of categories of loss such as consequential loss, loss of profit, loss of revenue, indirect loss, loss in connection with third party claims etc.;

- as a customer they must beware of 'consequential loss' exclusions as the meaning of the term is not clear;

- note that the words 'consequential loss including loss of profits' can be read down as not including direct loss that is loss of profits – broader words would exclude consequential loss *and* loss of profits;

- consider whether any liability should be excluded from the operation of the exclusion or limitation. It is usual to require liability for loss or damage suffered in connection with personal injury, death or property damage to be unlimited. Ideally for a customer, liability for breaching an intellectual property warranty or confidentiality obligation would also be unlimited;

- if an exclusion clause is in your favour then ideally it would expressly confirm it applies to liability for negligence as well as contract;

- consider the operation of statutes that may imply terms, or guarantee certain standards in connection with the supply of goods and services, that cannot be excluded, such as the *Competition and Consumer Act 2010* (Cth) – it may be that a broad exclusion does not take advantage of what is permitted under the Act and may even be illegal;

- ideally it would be clarified whether or not the limitations and exclusions apply to liability under any indemnities in the agreement;
- take note of 'exclusive remedies' which may also remove the ability to sue for damages for breach of the agreement;
- consider a incorporating a time bar (e.g. the other party cannot bring an action after 12 months following completion); and
- for completeness note the inability to exclude liability for contravention of section 18 of the Australian Consumer Law (schedule 2 to the *Competition and Consumer Act 2010* (Cth)).

www.ingramcontent.com/pod-product-compliance
Lightning Source LLC
Chambersburg PA
CBHW071122210326
41519CB00020B/6388